# Environmental Protection
## A Challenge Bigger Than All Outdoors

**By Michael deCourcy Hinds**

A Challenge
Bigger Than All Outdoors
# Environmental Protection

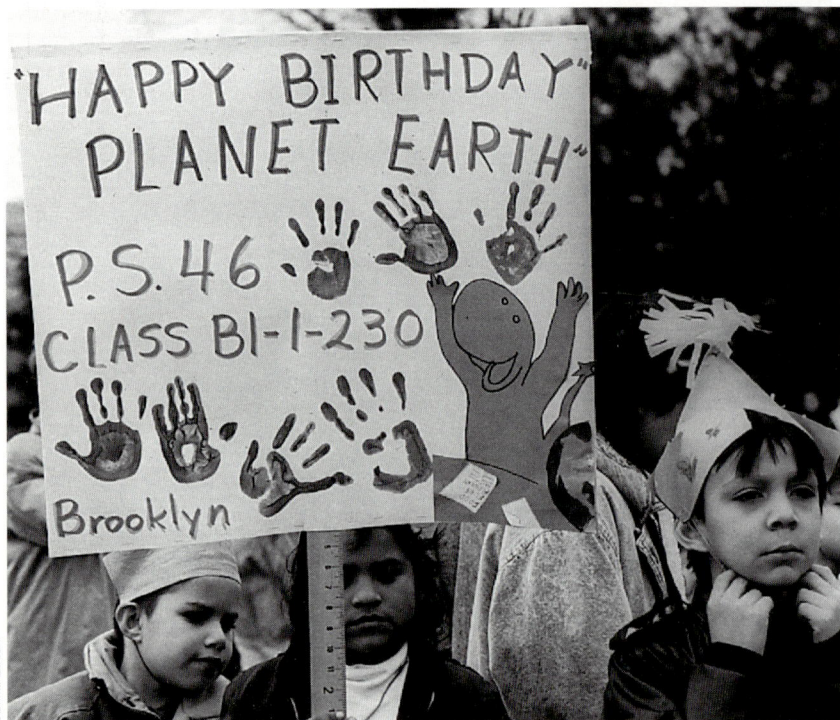

Gamma Liaison

**Earth Day, 1996**

Like housework, cleaning up the environment is a never-ending chore, increasing in volume as a family grows. ("I've never stopped loading this dishwasher ever since we got it," Erma Bombeck once complained.) When we began scrubbing the air in 1970, 74 million Americans were breathing tainted air and facing higher risks for cancer and for lung and heart diseases. In 1994, after spending hundreds of billions of dollars to reduce air pollution, 62 million Americans were still breathing air that failed to meet federal standards.

It's not that we've failed to make progress in reducing air pollution, it's that the chore has grown as the American family has grown; total population is up by 27 percent, and lifestyles have changed. For example, in 1970, Americans drove 1.1 trillion miles. In 1994, we drove twice as many miles, and our mileage may nearly double again by 2000. The growth in mileage simply outpaces the progress made in cleaning up tailpipe emissions, which produce more than half of all hazardous air pollution.

## Everyone Cares About the Environment

"We tolerate cancer-causing agents in our environment at our peril," wrote marine biologist Rachel Carson. She died of cancer in 1964, two years after her book, *Silent Spring*, became a bestseller and an inspiration for what was soon called the environmental movement. Today, strong public support for environmental protection has become part of American culture, incorporated into art, textbooks, and sitcom scripts. Eighty percent of Americans say they are active environmentalists or sympathetic toward environmental concerns, according to a 1994 Times Mirror survey; one in four Americans, across every demographic group, even selects "environmentalist" as the perfect self-description.

We've made gains in environmental protection, and we should do more, Americans tell pollsters. Yet few people see the issue as urgent – only 1 percent of Americans told Princeton Research in 1995 that the environment is the nation's most pressing problem. An overwhelming majority of Americans support strong environmental regulations, and they told the Wirthlin Group in 1994 that economic growth did not have to be sacrificed for environmental quality. But in a 1995 survey by Yankelovich Partners, most people agreed with the statement that "given our other problems right now" it would be better to go slow in "spending money to clean up the environment."

Although public opinion surveys demonstrate that Americans are deeply committed to a safe and healthy environment, surveys provide no clear answers about how to reach that goal or what tradeoffs people will accept, conclude Everett Carll Ladd and Karlyn H. Bowman in their 1995 booklet, *Attitudes Toward the Environment*.

## Where Do We Go From Here?

State and federal legislators are wrangling over how much money to budget for environmental protection and how to spend it. In 1995 and early 1996, congressional leaders campaigned to alter many environmental laws governing such things as endangered species, drinking water, toxic waste sites, pesticides, and grazing and logging on public lands. The leaders said regulations were too inflexible, needlessly costly, and focused too much on punishing polluters rather than seeking their cooperation. The complaints resonated with many Americans, but the proposed reforms struck many, both Republicans and Democrats, as going so far that they seemed anti-environmental. The House passed some legislation, but it went nowhere in the Senate.

House Speaker Newt Gingrich said that, in retrospect, it had been a mistake to sponsor such an aggressive reform campaign without first reassuring Americans that government continues to support environmental protection. In an April 1996 speech, given in an apparent effort to prepare the nation for the next round of reform proposals, Gingrich pledged allegiance to the environmental ethic: "The environmental movement in its values was basically right and in its goals was exactly right."

Environmental protection is a big, complex issue. Discussions inevitably fall back on scientific studies, but environmental science is rapidly evolving, and scientists often disagree. Americans must also consider their own views and values in deciding what approach the nation should take in environmental policy. Concerns such as the role of government, the costs of protection, human and

**The Rising Cost of Pollution Control: Spending to reduce all pollutants**

Consumer, government, and business expenditures on air, water, and solid waste pollution control and abatement in billions of dollars, 1972-1993

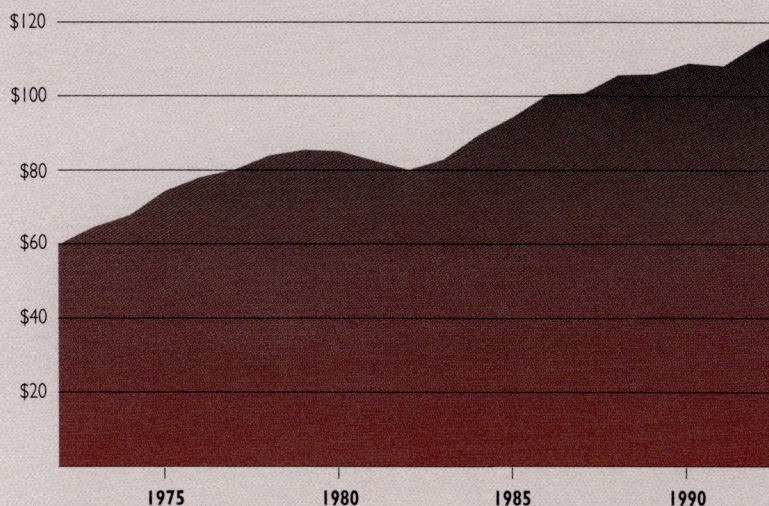

Source: Bureau of Economic Analysis

environmental health, and even the fate of the planet may play a part.

Most Americans live in an environment that, on many fronts, is cleaner than it was at any time in the past 50 years. For example, families can now fish in Ohio's Cuyahoga River, which was so polluted with oil and debris in 1969 that a spark from a passing train set the river ablaze. Since 1972, we have nearly doubled the number of swimmable and fishable lakes and rivers; yet more than 30 percent are still unusable for those purposes, according to the U.S. Environmental Protection Agency (EPA).

So is the glass half empty or half full? This question drives debates over many public issues, and none more than the environmental debate. Environmentalists not only differ in how they see the condition of the world, they disagree about whether the environment is getting better or worse and, in either case, what to do about it.

Today, as climatologists discuss the possibility of environmental disasters being caused by global warming, it seems quaint that just 40 years ago Americans told pollsters that littering was a serious environmental problem. Environmental perspectives, now more sophisticated and varied, range from

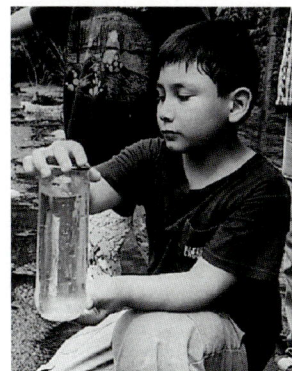

Environmental protection has become part of American culture – and many school courses.

New cars are much cleaner than old cars, but environmental gains have been undermined by Americans' driving bigger vehicles longer distances at higher speeds.

local and regional concerns to national and international conditions. Dividing priorities still further, Americans may be primarily concerned about land use, air quality, or water issues.

In considering what overall environmental approach to take, Americans have to consider some tough questions:

■ How clean is clean? Should we try to remove all pollution, or stop at some point when the cleaning bill seems high?

■ Is our money best spent controlling and cleaning up pollution – or preventing farmers, companies, and consumers from polluting in the first place?

■ Is the environment one among equal public challenges, or is it the most important one?

■ Should environmental concerns take precedence over the rights of property owners and over jobs in mining, logging, and ranching?

■ How far ahead should we look? Should we focus on clear and present dangers, or should we consider uncertain threats looming on the horizon?

## What Science Tells Us

As we struggle with these questions, science provides only partial answers, and the answers change considerably over relatively short periods. In 1975,

for example, a headline in *The New York Times* stated, "Scientists Ponder Why the World's Climate Is Changing: Major Cooling Widely Considered to Be Inevitable." In 1995, a *Times* headline said, "Scientists Say Earth's Warming Could Set Off Wide Disruptions." (Some scientists still cite evidence that the Earth is cooling.)

Environmental science is a slippery slope and the media often slip in news reports, adding to public confusion, according to a 1993 survey of 401 cancer specialists conducted by Roper Center for Public Opinion Research. Only 5 percent of the specialists say the nation's television network news programs are "highly reliable" in their reporting on the environmental causes of cancer, and only 10 percent of them consider the news weeklies highly reliable. These specialists say news coverage tends to overestimate cancer risks posed by man-made substances and to underestimate those posed by natural materials.

Government assesses risks and then sets environmental standards to reduce the risks to acceptable levels. What's considered acceptable is a subjective judgement, influenced by public pressures to reduce environmental risks as much as technology permits. But as cleanup costs rise, questions arise about how much money we should spend trying to reduce health risks. One federal standard for chloroform in tap water, for example, seeks to reduce the estimated risk of death to 6 in 10 million, which is one-fifth the estimated cancer risk that some people assume by eating peanut butter daily.

"It's confusing," says Neil D. Weinstein, a professor of human ecology and psychology at Rutgers University. "A public official might like us to consider all the risk possibilities and put them in order of magnitude, but the fact is, these numbers are very hard to obtain, very hard to understand, and the experts themselves don't agree on the numbers."

After considerable publicity about radon gas, for example, the government warned Americans in 1988 that their homes may be collecting dangerous amounts of this naturally occurring gas, which is odorless, tasteless, and invisible. Radon, produced by the decay of uranium in soil and rocks, is believed to cause about 20,000 lung cancer deaths a year, making it one of the most significant cancer risks in the environment. But Americans, surveyed by the Roper Organization that year, ranked radon

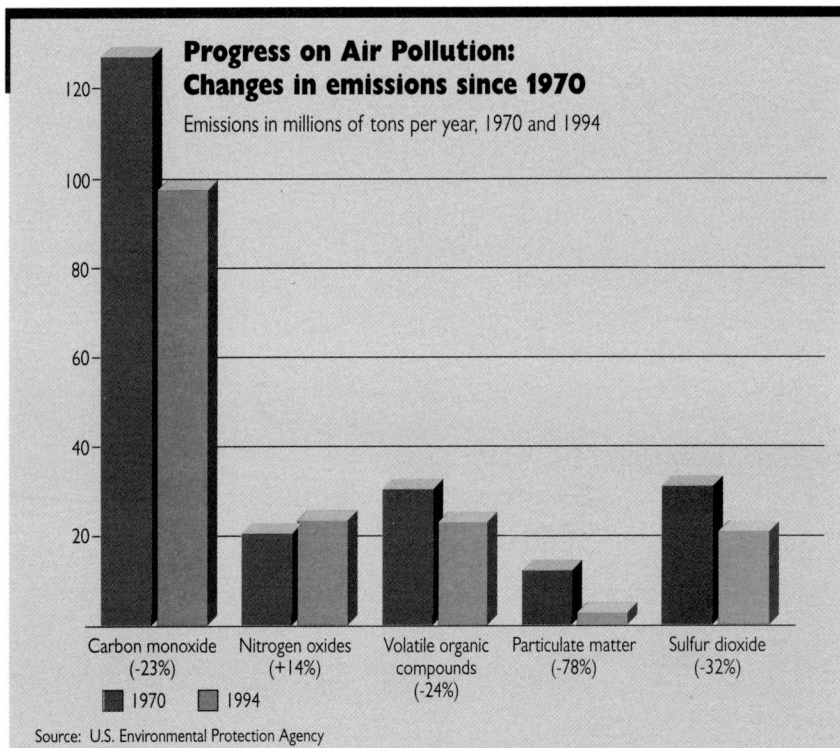

## Progress on Air Pollution:
## Changes in emissions since 1970

Emissions in millions of tons per year, 1970 and 1994

| | Carbon monoxide (-23%) | Nitrogen oxides (+14%) | Volatile organic compounds (-24%) | Particulate matter (-78%) | Sulfur dioxide (-32%) |

■ 1970   ■ 1994

Source: U.S. Environmental Protection Agency

27th out of 28 hazards, just below medical X-rays and above microwave ovens. Today, most Americans are still unconvinced of the hazard posed by radon, and scientists, too, have raised doubts, with some saying that the radon risk is much lower than had been originally thought or may apply only to cigarette smokers. These kinds of risk assessments involve three major problems:

First, unless historical data can precisely quantify a risk, risk estimates are only scientific guesses. They are often extrapolated from clinical tests that involve administering massive doses of suspect substances to rodents over a short period – leaving open to question the impact of extremely small doses on human health over a lifetime.

Second, emotions and social customs, more than mathematical ratios, govern responses to warnings of risk. Studies show that people worry about man-made risks more than natural ones, new risks more than familiar ones, visible risks more than invisible ones, and uncontrollable risks more than those they have some control over.

Third, people are not equally exposed to the same risk factors, and their ability to avoid risks often depends on their income level and where they live. For example, poor people who live in New York's South Bronx, which has many recycling and waste-processing plants, have a high rate of asthma. Nationally, black children are four times more likely to die from asthma than white children, the federal Centers for Disease Control and Prevention reported in 1996.

### A note to the reader about NIF books

Each book in this series for the National Issues Forums outlines an issue and several approaches, or choices, that address a problem and its solution. Rather than conforming to any single public proposal, each choice reflects widely held, but contrasting, concerns and principles. Panels of experts review manuscripts to make sure the choices are presented accurately and fairly.

Unlike most periodicals, issue books do not identify individuals or organizations with partisan labels such as Democrat, Republican, conservative, or liberal. The goal is to present ideas in a fresh way that encourages readers to judge them on their merit. Issue books include quotations from experts and public officials when their views appear consistent with the principles of a choice. But these quoted individuals might not endorse every aspect of a choice as it is described here.

Assessing environmental risks involves a lot of scientific guesswork.

### A Framework for Discussion

To prime discussion, this issue book presents three perspectives on the direction the nation should take regarding environmental protection:

■ **Choice One** says the government has made much progress in environmental protection, but much more needs to be done. Government must strengthen laws and enforcement even if, to keep costs down, regulations are made more flexible.

■ **Choice Two** says that burdensome regulations – at all levels of government – dampen economic growth, infringe on property rights, and produce poor environmental results. Incentives, not regulations, provide more effective environmental protection, in this view.

■ **Choice Three** says pollution is threatening our health and destroying the planet. Government must aggressively regulate pollutants and wean industries and consumers from environmentally destructive practices, products, and lifestyles.

### For Further Reading/Environmental Protection

■ Ronald Bailey, ed., *The True State of the Planet* (New York: The Free Press, 1995).

■ Lester R. Brown, *State of the World 1996* (New York: W.W. Norton & Company, 1996).

■ Theodore D. Goldfarb, ed., *Taking Sides: Clashing Views on Controversial Environmental Issues* (Guilford, Conn.: The Dushkin Publishing Group, 1995).

# Strengthening Laws and Enforcement

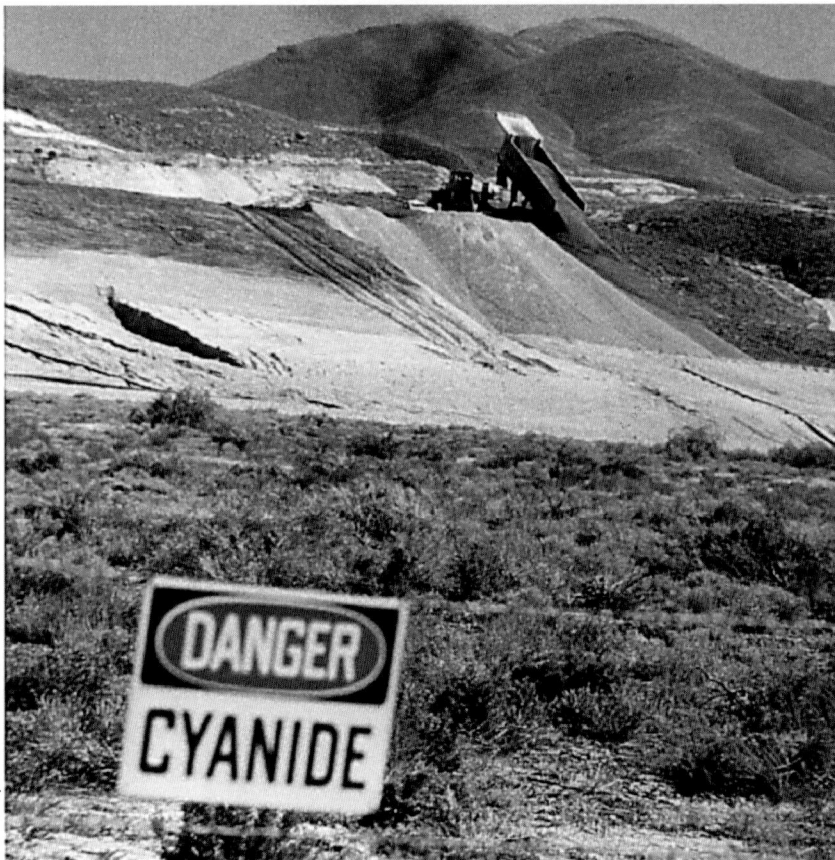

Mineral Policy Center

**Mining companies buy public land for a pittance, haul away mineral treasures, and often leave behind environmental disasters like this one in Nevada.**

In the Independence Mountain Range in Nevada, where a new gold rush is churning through the wilderness, a lone aspen tree stands at a dusty crossroads in Jerritt Canyon. "Goodbye" is carved into its bark. Here, and on other federal land held in trust for Americans, the law of the land seems to have been written for *Ripley's Believe It or Not.*

The General Mining Law of 1872, which Western lawmakers repeatedly defend at the behest of mining companies, says that anyone who finds valuable minerals on public land can keep them. The law requires the federal government to sell some of the most valuable public lands for $2.50 to $5 an acre to prospectors and speculators. Many of the buyers are foreign; in 1994, for example, a Canadian company paid $10,000 for land containing an estimated $10 billion in gold deposits. U.S. Interior Secretary Bruce Babbitt reluctantly approved the sale, calling it "the biggest gold heist since the days of Butch Cassidy."

But it gets worse. No environmental concerns can impede a sale, and the law doesn't require the purchaser to restore lands to their pre-mining condition. Companies annually extract up to $4 billion worth of gold and other hardrock minerals, but they pay no royalties. Gold miners use a chemical process – developed by the government – that tends to pollute waterways with cyanide-laced runoff. Miners are supposed to comply with environmental laws, but federal courts have never levied the maximum penalties, a $250,000 fine or five years in prison, or both. When the ore is gone, companies abandon their mines, often leaving behind environmental disasters, including 4,000 waste-filled sites in national parks alone.

## Stronger Laws, Better Enforcement

The 1872 law is the most egregious example of what's wrong with our laws, according to the Choice One perspective on environmental protection. In this view, we should repeal the 1872 mining law as part of an effort to overhaul our laws protecting the environment. Over the last 25 years, the federal government has made much progress in cleaning up the environment. We have many good laws, but many need to be improved. Compliance has also been spotty, and enforcement is frequently feeble, in this view.

Much work needs to be done. We should strengthen both environmental laws and their enforcement, in this view. Take drinking water as an example. The government says that drinking water poses one of the nation's top health risks, yet it budgets a total of only $150 million a year for the EPA to conduct research, develop standards, subsidize and monitor state programs, and enforce standards on groundwater pollution. That represents less than 1 percent of the agency's enforcement budget for all environmental regulations.

Paradoxically, while the government is cutting corners on making tap water safe, consumer concerns about tainted water have helped push sales of water filters and bottled water to $7.7 billion in 1995, up from $3.1 billion in 1988, according to industry statistics. There is ample reason for concern.

In March 1993, a protozoan parasite called cryptosporidium invaded Milwaukee's water system, causing illness in 400,000 people and killing 104 people, including a 4-year-old, Rebecca Furmann. The young, the old, and people with medical problems are the first to succumb to tainted tap water. Milwaukee's outbreak was unusual only in its intensity; 45 million Americans rely on water systems that, at some point, contained cryptosporidia, according to studies based on government data.

But the EPA does not require water systems to test for the parasite, and many do not. What's the holdup? By law, the agency must prove that the health benefits of instituting a regulation outweigh the costs. A frustrated Carol Browner, the EPA administrator, asks: "Does the public want us to require some sort of protection now, given what happened in Milwaukee, or does it want us to wait

## What Can Be Done?

### Supporters of Choice One generally favor the following measures:

■ Government must continue setting standards that seek to reduce pollution to a minimum.

■ Congress must substantially increase funding for the Environmental Protection Agency, especially in view of the budget reductions since 1995.

■ Government must substantially strengthen enforcement of environmental regulations, and allocate resources so that the most critical problems get the most attention.

■ To cope with increasing auto pollution, government must make it a national priority to develop pollution-free vehicles. Government must also enact stricter emissions standards, and enforce them.

■ Improving management of public lands and waterways must be made a national priority. The 1872 mining law, a national disgrace, must be repealed.

■ With money tight, government must create more flexible and efficient regulations, producing the most environmental protection possible for each dollar spent by government, industry, and citizens; whenever feasible, this means setting strict standards and leaving it up to the marketplace to find the best way to comply.

years and years until we know everything there is to know about the problem?" Choice One calls for regulation now.

Better standards and more federal enforcement are clearly needed. Shortly after the Milwaukee outbreak, the General Accounting Office, a congressional agency, reported that most water inspection programs were in shambles. "It is fair enough to say that without improvement in the states' sanitary programs, consumers run a higher risk of being confronted with contaminated water," Steve L. Elstein, an author of the agency study, told *The New York Times.*

The Centers for Disease Control estimates that polluted tap water annually sickens 940,000 people, often with flu-like symptoms, and kills 900. At some time, one in five Americans drink tap water that does not meet federal standards for such things as fecal contamination, parasites, and pesticides. As a result, the federal agency advises people

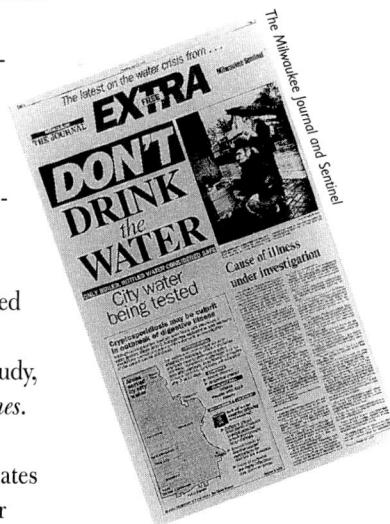

April 8, 1993: *The Milwaukee Journal and Sentinel* warns residents about parasites in the drinking water.

## A Tainted Water Supply:
## Drinking water that violates federal standards

Water violations reported to the EPA, 1994-1995

| Type of contaminant or problem | Number of water systems violating standards | Population affected by violation |
|---|---|---|
| Fecal coliform bacteria (E. coli) | 2,726 | 11.9 million |
| Inadequate disinfection/failure to filter | 1,478 | 20 million |
| Chemical contaminants (includes pesticides and industrial contaminants, nitrates, radioactive contaminants, and trihalomethanes) | 1,050 | 2.3 million |
| Lead | 1,007 | 2 million |

Source: Environmental Working Group

### The Outdated Mining Law: Giving away our national resources

Amount paid by companies for federal land and the taxpayer loss, based on the estimated value of minerals on the land

| Name of mine, State | Owner, Country | Mineral | Price | Taxpayer loss |
|---|---|---|---|---|
| Goldstrike, NY | American Barrick, Canada | Gold | $5,190 | $10,200,000,000 |
| Montanore, MT | Noranda Minerals, Canada | Copper, silver | $185 | $3,688,200,000 |
| Stillwater, MT | Chevron, U.S. Manville, U.S. | Platinum, palladium | $12,660 | $3,378,300,000 |
| Mount Emmons, CO | Cyprus-Amax, U.S. | Molybdenum | $1,000 | $2,999,200,000 |
| Helvetia, AZ | Asarco, U.S. | Copper, silver | $3,470 | $1,848,500,000 |
| McCoy/Cove, NV | Echo Bay Mines, Canada | Gold, silver | $3,305 | $1,448,600,000 |
| Twin Creeks, NV | Santa Fe Pacific, U.S. | Gold | $3,520 | $1,402,500,000 |
| Brush Wellman, UT | Brush Wellman, U.S. | Beryllium | $8,830 | $1,268,300,000 |
| Jerritt Canyon, NV | Anglo-American, S. Africa FMC, U.S. | Gold | $5,080 | $1,113,200,000 |
| Sanchez, AZ | AZCO, U.S. | Copper | $1,640 | $1,052,800,000 |

Source: Mineral Policy Center

with immune-system deficiencies, including AIDS, to boil or filter their tap water.

Clearly, say Choice One supporters, to protect our health and the environment, government must do a better job regulating and enforcing regulations that clean up the water, air, and land.

### Protect Public Lands

The federal government has greatly expanded national parks and substantially reduced the rate at which wetlands are lost to development and farming. But the government, which owns a third of all U.S. land, including half of the acreage in the West, has a poor record in land management. Consider these examples:

■ Mismanagement of public land is actually encouraged by many regulations and laws, including the 1872 mining law, leaving behind expensive problems. Cleaning up abandoned mines on public lands, as well as 10,000 miles of streams polluted by mine waste, could cost taxpayers

Overgrazing is the number one cause of degradation of fisheries and watersheds in the West.

between $32 billion and $72 billion, according to the Mineral Policy Center, a research organization in Washington.

■ Selective logging provides wood products and creates jobs. But government must stop subsidizing timber sales and logging practices, which cost taxpayers hundreds of millions of dollars a year – and lead to soil erosion, deforestation, and the extinction of species.

■ Overgrazing is considered the number one cause of degradation to fisheries and watersheds in the West. But environmentalists' surveys indicate that the government subsidizes overgrazing on up to 177 million acres of public pasture. One of many federal subsidies: the government charges ranchers only $1.31 a month for each cow they feed and water on public lands. One inevitable result is that ranchers tend to raise more cattle than the range can sustain.

Underpricing natural resources is a sure way to promote their abuse, in this view. And regardless of the economics, government should not permit a relatively small number of miners and loggers to destroy public lands that belong to all Americans.

> One of many federal subsidies: the government charges ranchers only $1.31 a month for each cow they feed and water on public lands.

### Be More Efficient

William Reilly, EPA administrator from 1987 to 1991, recently acknowledged that during his tenure only 30 percent of the agency's budget was devoted to high-risk environmental pollutants. That means we're not being efficient. Because cleaning up the environment is so costly, it's particularly important to get the most environmental protection for our money. Therefore, government must give the highest priority to the highest-risk problems and regulate all pollutants in the most efficient way possible. Too often, government creates inefficient regulations that not only set standards, but also specify the methods and even the equipment businesses must use to comply.

Public officials, environmental advocates, and business executives have already found a better solution: flexible regulations. With this approach, government sets standards and businesses comply in the most economic way. The 1990 Clean Air

Act provides a model for this kind of regulation. One provision of the law deals with the pollutant sulphur dioxide, which mixes with clouds to form acid rain. The law calls for cutting in half the 20 million tons of sulphur dioxide emitted by the nation's utilities and factories by 2000. But, unlike most environmental regulations, this law does not insist that each company cut power-plant emissions in half. Rather, the law gives individual companies great flexibility in how they comply as long as the national goal is reached. As a result, the estimated compliance costs are cut in half without compromising the law's environmental goal. This also turns what could have been a regulatory burden into an opportunity for companies to make money by doing an especially good job, reducing emissions by more than federal standards require.

Here is how the system works. Companies earn "pollution credits" when they reduce emissions to levels below federal air quality standards, usually by more than half of their former levels; they can sell the credits to another company or use them later. To comply with the law, a company has several options, including burning coal with a lower sulphur content, removing the pollutant with smokestack scrubbers – or buying "pollution credits" from other companies. Illinois Power Company, for example, decided to invest in a smokestack scrubber, reducing the plant's emissions to only 6,000 tons of sulphur dioxide a year from 89,300 tons in 1985. That drastic reduction in pollution earned the company credits for 34,834 tons of pollution, which the company can sell to another company at rates between $200 and $500 a ton, according to market demand. Buyers might include a utility that finds it less expensive to buy pollution credits than to repair an old power plant that's scheduled for replacement.

The government subsidizes logging on public land, such as this clear-cut forest on the Olympic Peninsula in Washington.

## Spending on the Environment:

### A small slice of the federal pie

Federal outlays in billions of dollars, 1970-1995

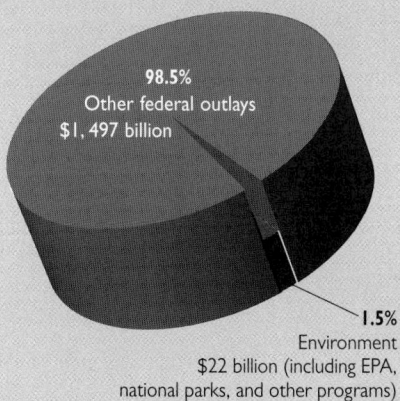

98.5%
Other federal outlays
$1, 497 billion

1.5%
Environment
$22 billion (including EPA, national parks, and other programs)

Source: Federal Budget of the United States, Fiscal Year 1997

### A wavering commitment

EPA appropriations in billions of 1995 dollars, 1970-1995

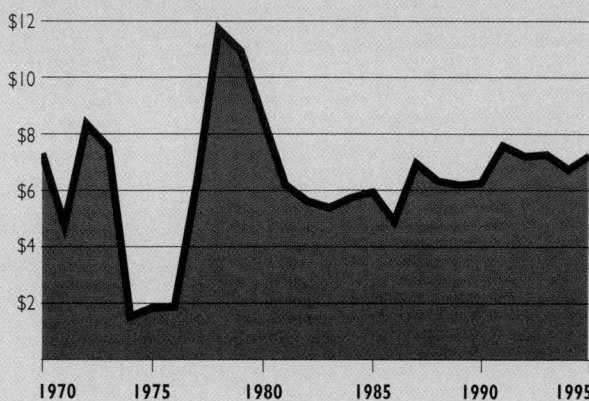

Source: U.S. Environmental Protection Agency

## In Support

✓ The government has made significant progress, but needs to do much more. The Clean Water Act, for example, called for all surface waters to be swimmable and fishable by 1983; but now, 13 years past the target date, more than a third of our waters are still unusable for those purposes.

✓ There is widespread public support for reducing pollution to the minimum level possible and, to achieve this goal, government should develop much stricter environmental regulations. For example, many environmental regulations seek to reduce pollution at the smokestack, sewer outlet, and tailpipe. But government is doing relatively little to reduce the vast amount of polluted runoff from farms, suburban lawns, and city streets.

✓ Environmental progress has been slowed by inadequate enforcement of many regulations. Each year, for example, tens of thousands of serious violations of the drinking water regulations occur, yet enforcement actions have been exceedingly rare, according to environmentalists' reviews of government data. For everyone's good, government should step up enforcement.

✓ We can get the most environmental protection for each dollar we spend by giving businesses more flexibility in complying with regulations. Research at Colby College suggests that compliance costs associated with conventional regulations are, on average, six times higher than compliance costs associated with flexible regulations.

✓ To be effective, government should practice what it preaches about the environment. By undervaluing and mismanaging natural resources, government has encouraged abuse of public lands, leading to extensive environmental problems.

## In Opposition

✓ This approach does not go nearly far enough, according to some critics. For one thing, it focuses too much on managing pollution and too little on effective programs to prevent it.

✓ Choice One also puts too little emphasis on global environmental threats. If we don't address them soon, they will be much more difficult to address later on.

✓ This approach calls for regulations that reduce costs by giving businesses flexibility, but that flexibility has human costs. Under the 1990 Clean Air Act, for example, people will continue to face health risks if nearby utilities buy "pollution credits" instead of cleaning up pollution. Pollution, then, may become concentrated in some areas, most likely in areas where the poor live. It's better to have all companies reduce pollution equally so everyone benefits.

✓ According to another group of opponents, this approach overstates most environmental problems, which have been solved or are being solved. Since 1973, for example, the number of metropolitan areas failing to meet clean air standards declined by almost 90 percent.

✓ This approach assumes that pollution is the cause of many ills, but scientists do not really know what causes many human diseases, such as cancer. Many environmental regulations are based on wildly expensive guesses.

✓ Choice One seeks to fine-tune a regulatory approach that needs to be scrapped entirely. The most effective and efficient way to protect the environment is to deregulate it.

### For Further Reading/
Strengthening Laws and Enforcement

■ Marc K. Landy, Marc J. Roberts, and Stephen R. Thomas, *The Environmental Protection Agency: Asking the Wrong Questions From Nixon to Clinton* (New York: Oxford University Press, 1994).

■ Paul R. Portney, ed., *Public Policies for Environmental Protection* (Washington, D.C.: Resources for the Future, 1990).

■ Kirkpatrick Sale, *The Green Revolution: The American Environmental Movement 1962-1992* (New York: Hill and Wang, 1993).

# Using Incentives, Not Regulations

Uniphoto

Dan Newton, with his children, Joe, Trisha, and Jessica, in their Douglas County, Oregon, forest.

**M**any people put their retirement savings in stocks and bonds, but Dan Newton put his in trees. A forester who has won awards for his stewardship of private timberland, Dan scraped together family funds and bank loans in the early 1980s to buy 160 acres of timberland near his home in Douglas County, Oregon. He and his wife, Kathy, weeded, fertilized, and planted an additional 40,000 Douglas firs – all with an eye to logging timber and replanting trees in about 20 years.

Then, in 1993, the federal government stepped in, proposing to preserve the Newtons' property as, essentially, a bird sanctuary. It seemed that a northern spotted owl, a species listed as threatened with extinction, had nested 1,000 feet from their property.

"We were outraged that the federal government was proposing to take our property away without any compensation," said Newton, who estimates its worth at about $300,000 today.

Even though the federal government already owns half the timberland in Oregon, Newton said, the government is seeking to restrict logging on thousands of privately owned parcels near spotted owl nests. The proposal, which Newton and others are fighting, would set aside up to 1,800 acres of privately owned forest, with timber valued at up to $18 million, for each owl nest.

## The Problem: Regulatory Overkill

By devaluing the Newtons' property without providing fair compensation, the government is essentially stealing it, violating their constitutional rights, and creating enormous economic hardship for them, according to Choice Two supporters. It's immoral and undemocratic. Besides, property owners are better environmental stewards than regulators, because they have emotional and financial ties to the land, in this view. The Newtons' experience also illustrates how government is becoming less concerned with protecting people from an unhealthy environment and more concerned with protecting a healthy environment from people.

Regulatory overkill, occurring at all levels of government, oppresses businesses, landowners, and, indirectly, all Americans, who pay inflated prices for almost everything to cover billions of dollars a year that companies spend complying with burdensome environmental regulations. Three examples:

■ The Clean Water Act sets the utopian goal of "zero discharge" of pollutants into all navigable bodies of water.

# What Can Be Done?

## Supporters of Choice Two generally favor the following measures:

■ We must reduce, to the absolute minimum, the role of government – at all levels – in managing environmental resources. We must replace most regulations with what works best in America: the free-market system, which relies on individual responsibility and financial interests to protect the environment. We also have the courts to hold polluters accountable.

■ Environmental protection laws must focus on protecting human health, not the health of every rare bug or plant. Stop wasteful programs that try to protect the environment from us.

■ Government should conduct an economic impact statement for existing regulations and any new environmental proposals. We do not need stricter efficiency standards for automobiles, for example, because the gains would be insignificant and the costs very significant.

■ To promote better stewardship of the environment, government should put more public land in private hands. Private individuals and companies have a stronger interest than the government in taking good care of the land.

■ Government should use incentives, not regulations, to encourage property owners to provide land for use as habitats of rare species. When it's absolutely necessary to restrict the use of private land, government must compensate the owner for the loss.

■ The Safe Drinking Water Act requires cities like Columbus, Ohio, to spend $24,000 a year testing municipal water supplies for 43 pesticides it knows it won't find, including one that, since 1979, has been used only on pineapples in Hawaii.

■ The cost of complying with regulations has slowed economic growth by a significant percentage, an average of 0.2 percent a year between 1974 and 1985, according to a 1990 study at Harvard.

What's more, the government's heavy-handed approach to environmental protection is wasteful, producing gains that are marginal, at best, in this view. Thanks to federal regulations, for example, the nation's schools are spending up to $200 billion to remove

The Endangered Species Act protects this kangaroo rat as well as many other species of insects, spiders, snails, and bats.

asbestos from their buildings. Yet federal statistics suggest that the tiny risk of a student dying from football injuries is up to 2,000 times greater than the even tinier risk of a student dying from cancer after attending schools constructed with asbestos.

"The United States is attempting to produce environmental benefits in much the same way that the former Soviet Union attempted to produce wheat – through government command and control of all relevant resources," the Competitive Enterprise Institute, a research organization in Washington, says in a 1994 report. "This produces some environmental improvements, just as the Soviet Union produced some wheat. But both approaches inevitably fail to meet the demands placed upon them."

The problem is government, and the solution is deregulation, in this view. Thousands of federal, state, and local regulations should be scrapped, and others should be reformed so that they use incentives, rather than penalties, to encourage compliance. And, in this view, there is no need for regulatory agencies to enforce many environmental laws, because citizens and property owners can use existing liability laws to hold environmental abusers accountable in court.

## What About Human Habitat?

Since when does human habitat get less consideration than the habitat of a northern spotted owl or kangaroo rat, this choice asks. Since the passage and subsequent amendment of the Endangered Species Act of 1966. One federal judge described the act as "the strongest piece of land use legislation in history." Initially, the law was widely viewed as an uncontroversial, low-cost effort to rescue some spectacular animals like whooping cranes and grizzly bears. It required federal agencies to protect an estimated 80 endangered or threatened species and their habitats on federal lands.

But regulations have a way of spinning out of control, say supporters of this view. By 1992, regulatory agencies had listed 895 species of flora and fauna (including the Tuna Cave cockroach, Coffin Cave mold beetle, and silver rice rats), and were considering listing 3,941 others. And now, prompted by lawsuits from environmental advocates, federal agencies are restricting or proposing restrictions on private as well as public land to protect these species. This is

Private landowners, not regulators, are the best environmental stewards.

an egregious violation of citizens' constitutional right to "just compensation" when government takes their property for public use, say Choice Two supporters, including many legal scholars. However, the courts have so far upheld these restrictions.

Not only does this kind of law violate property rights, it costs many people their jobs. After the northern spotted owl was listed as "threatened" in 1991, the government proposed or designated more than 30 million acres of public and private woodlands in California and the Pacific Northwest as a protected habitat for the owl. Restrictions on logging have already closed hundreds of sawmills and related businesses, devastating many rural communities like Forks, Washington, a town of 2,800, where job losses are associated with many distressing statistics. Between September 1990 and September 1991, for example, the number of families on welfare rose by 64 percent, the number of people receiving food from a local food bank rose by 66 percent, and domestic abuse increased by 96 percent.

Nationally, as timber harvests decreased, prices for many wood products soared, draining the economy of $20 billion, according to one study, and increasing the cost of a new home by as much as $2 per square foot of floor area, according to another study. "Saving the owl had effectively shut down an area larger than Massachusetts, Vermont, New Hampshire, and Connecticut combined, costing the economy tens of billions of dollars and casting tens of thousands out of work," Alston Chase summarizes in his 1995 book, *In a Dark Wood: The Fight Over Forests and the Rising Tyranny of Ecology*.

It would be one thing if the sacrifice made sense. Choice Two supporters note that many scientists consider the owl habitat regulations and numerous other environmental rules to be unscientific, counterproductive, and wasteful. For example, the initial government decision to proscribe logging $10 billion worth of mature and dying trees in 1977 was based on a graduate student's study of 12 owls that he had fitted with radio transmitters, Chase writes. The push for preservation by advocacy groups snowballed over the years despite mounting evidence that there were thousands of spotted owls, not merely hundreds, and that the owls nested in young trees and clear-cut areas as well as in mature and dying trees. Not surprisingly, such ill-founded regulations can backfire. Without logging to remove dying and dried-out trees, forests are more susceptible to fire, which in 1988 alone consumed 5 million acres of timber and wildlife habitat, according to a 1994 report from the National Commission on Wildlife Disasters. "Public concern for

## The Endangered Species Act: Many listed, few saved

Number of endangered and threatened species on 1996 list: **959**

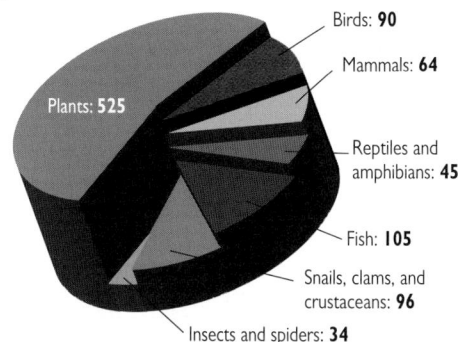

Plants: 525
Birds: 90
Mammals: 64
Reptiles and amphibians: 45
Fish: 105
Snails, clams, and crustaceans: 96
Insects and spiders: 34

Number of endangered and threatened species removed from list since passage of Act in 1966: **26**

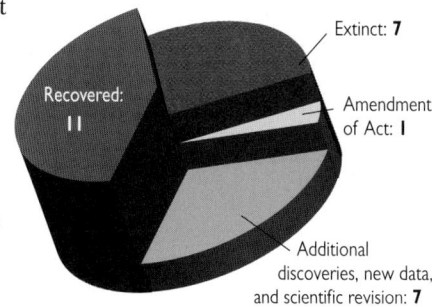

Recovered: 11
Extinct: 7
Amendment of Act: 1
Additional discoveries, new data, and scientific revision: 7

Source: U.S. Fish and Wildlife Service

## The Abundance of Resources: Forest growth exceeds harvesting

U.S. timber growth and harvests in billions of cubic feet, 1920-1991

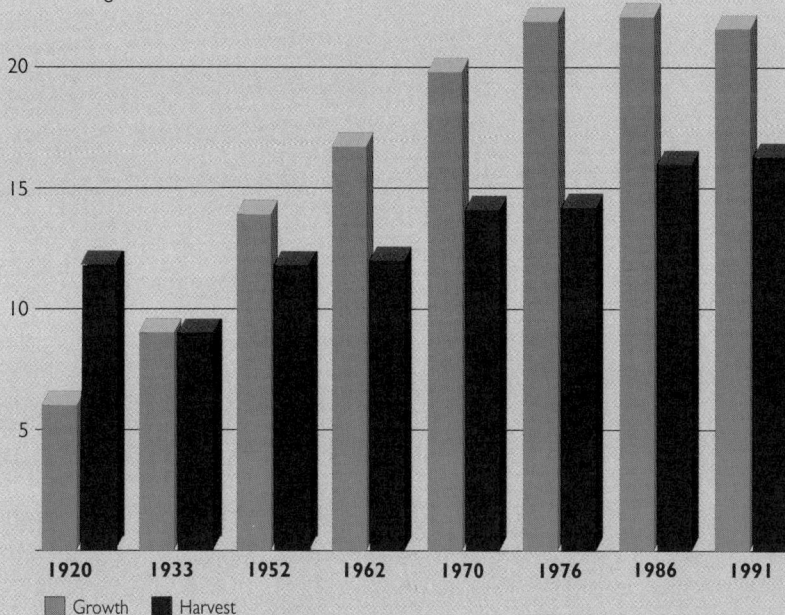

Growth    Harvest

Source: U.S. Forest Service

Danny Snyder

With the closing of coal mines, unemployment in Marion County, West Virginia, jumped to 9 percent, and 27 stores closed, including many on Adams Street in Fairmont, giving it the look of a ghost town.

"What am I going to do? I'm scared to death," John Beveridge told *The New York Times*. He and 367 other miners lost their jobs when their mine closed due to environmental restrictions on burning coal.

endangered species," the federal commission concluded, "may not always achieve the desired goal."

## Small Benefits, Big Costs

Many environmental laws exact huge financial and human costs, but provide minimal or uncertain benefits, in this view. The 1990 Clean Air Act, for example, calls for sharp reductions in the emission of sulphur dioxide, a compound linked to acid rain. But early assessments of the damage caused

by acid rain have been widely discredited, according to many recent scientific studies, which indicate that the acid rain presents "no or minimal damage" to human or environmental health, Robert Owen Rye writes in "The Effects of Acid Rain," a chapter in the 1995 book, *But Is It True? A Citizen's Guide to Environmental Health and Safety Issues*.

For coal miners, their families, and rural communities east of the Mississippi, this is not just an academic debate. "What am I going to do? I'm scared to death," John Beveridge told *The New York Times* in February 1996. He and 367 other miners lost their jobs when their mine closed, and he has almost no hope of finding another job that pays as well as mining – $48,000 in his last year. The mine is full of coal, but it's high-sulphur coal, and the number of buyers has dwindled since the 1990 law sharply reduced the amount of high-sulfur coal a utility can burn without installing expensive smokestack scrubbers. Unemployment in Marion County, West Virginia, jumped to 9 percent in 1995, and 27 of the county's 355 stores closed. "Conditions across most of the Eastern coal country are the bleakest since the Great Depression," *The Times* reported, adding that nearly 1,000 coal mines in the region have closed since 1990.

Since environmental laws have the potential to harm families and communities without producing many benefits, Choice Two supporters say the government should conduct an economic impact statement for all current and proposed regulations.

### The Quest for Perfect Safety: The high cost of regulating environmental risks

Estimated cost per life saved, computed by dividing total cost of enforcing regulation by estimated total number of lives potentially saved, 1991

| Regulation | Estimated cost per life potentially saved |
|---|---|
| Ban on unvented space heaters | $100,000 |
| Ban on flammable children's sleepwear | $100,000 |
| Asbestos exposure limit for workers | $8.3 million |
| Asbestos ban | $110 million |
| Ban on toxic waste disposal on land | $4.2 billion |
| Formaldehyde exposure limit for workers | $82 billion |

Source: U.S. Office of Management and Budget

## In Support

✓ Government efforts to regulate the environment are wasteful, often providing small benefits at enormous cost. By deregulating the environment, we can allow the market to provide the environmental benefits people want at a price they can afford. Years ago, the government decided that the airline and trucking industries were far too complicated to be regulated effectively; the environment is infinitely more complex than those industries, and it's time the government recognized it.

✓ Property owners are the best environmental stewards, because they have a keen self-interest in protecting the value of their property. Government should promote individual responsibility and private ownership by using fewer regulations and more incentives.

✓ When government restricts the use of private land, thus devaluing its worth, it is only fair to compensate the owners.

✓ Environmental protection should focus on human health, but the government is using more and more of our taxes in a wrongheaded effort to protect the environment from us.

✓ Costly environmental programs often attempt the impossible: to eliminate risks from life. If asbestos poses almost no risk to schoolchildren, the nation should not be required to spend $200 billion removing it from buildings.

✓ Environmental regulations drain the economy and eliminate jobs. Entire communities have been devastated by restrictions on logging, ranching, and mining. Studies indicate that the cost of complying with environmental regulations is slowing down economic growth.

## In Opposition

✓ Government took the lead in protecting the environment precisely because our water, air, and land were deteriorating under the free-market system.

✓ This approach dismisses significant threats. For example, many biologists consider the spotted owl to be an indicator species, its fragile status indicative of how many other species are faring. In 1995, the U.S. National Academy of Sciences endorsed, as scientifically sound, our current approach to protecting fragile species.

✓ This approach suggests that citizens, using the legal system, can take the place of regulatory agencies in stopping polluters, but it does not say how most people would gain the expertise to identify environmental problems or find the money to sue.

✓ Government has the authority to make property owners use their land in an environmentally safe way, the U.S. Supreme Court ruled in June 1995. People shouldn't be compensated for obeying the law.

✓ Environmental regulation has a mild, but positive, effect on jobs, according to a survey of national studies at Lewis and Clark College. The regulations caused less than one-tenth of 1 percent of all major layoffs (those involving more than 50 workers) from 1987 to 1990. But in 1992 alone, environmental protection and pollution abatement employed 4 million Americans, most in blue-collar jobs.

✓ Environmental laws rarely impede development. The federal Fish and Wildlife Service, for example, reports that, of 94,113 requests by landowners involving environmentally sensitive areas between 1987 and 1992, only 91 were denied, abandoned, or not resolved.

### For Further Reading/
Using Incentives, Not Regulations

■ Joseph L. Bast, Peter J. Hill, and Richard C. Rue, *Eco-Sanity: A Common-Sense Guide to Environmentalism* (Lanham, Md.: Madison Books, 1994).

■ Alston Chase, *In a Dark Wood: The Fight Over Forests and the Rising Tyranny of Ecology* (Boston: Houghton Mifflin Company, 1995).

■ Competitive Enterprise Institute, *Environmental Briefing Book for Congressional Candidates* (Washington, D.C.: Competitive Enterprise Institute, 1994).

Niculae Asciu

# Working Toward a Sustainable Environment

A typical scene in
Dade County, Florida, after
Hurricane Andrew in 1992.

**A**ndrew, a hurricane of Biblical
proportions, swept through Dade
County, Florida, on August 22, 1992.
With winds gusting up to 212 miles an
hour, the hurricane turned cars, trucks,
roofs, and entire fields of fruit trees into
airborne missiles that bombarded a
500-square-mile area. It attacked a population of about 2 million people, killing 13
and contributing to the deaths of 61 others.

In just four hours, Andrew caused $30 billion in
damage, partially or completely destroying 85,000
homes, leaving 250,000 people homeless, closing
6,000 businesses permanently, wiping out 65,000
jobs, and sending 25,000 people to mental health
clinics. "I cried every day for three months, I
thought I'd never stop," Pat Faris told *The New
York Times*, not long after a bulldozer pushed what
was left of her family's century-old farmhouse into
a heap of trash.

Scientists are not sure if Andrew, America's
most destructive hurricane, was stirred up by global
warming trends. But they say Andrew provides a
glimpse of the kind of destruction global warming
is likely to cause. Other glimpses include the stun-
ning number of record-breaking floods, blizzards,
and heat waves we've seen during the last 15 years.

## Global Problems, Sustainable Solutions

Choice Three supporters take the long view, considering the nation's environmental health in terms
of the global ecosystem. And they say it doesn't
look good: pollution is threatening our health and
destroying the planet. But they're optimistic, saying the solution is at hand and includes sensible
things like replanting forests, relying more on solar
energy, and expanding public transportation. The
solution, however, includes major changes in our
no-deposit-no-return lifestyle. In this view, the
environment simply cannot absorb the rising
amount of pollution that pours out of the exhaust
pipes of our increasingly large vans and pickup
trucks; and the environment simply cannot regenerate if we continue to harvest natural resources at
today's furious pace.

In this view, government must go much further
than the Choice One approach, which strengthens
laws and their enforcement to reduce the pollution
that's choking us today. We must not only increase
cleanup efforts, we must prevent pollution from
occurring in the first place, with stricter regulations
and higher taxes on polluting products.

Effective environmental protection, then, requires that we lower consumption and pollution to levels that can be sustained, generation after generation. And since we, as Americans, use a disproportionate share of the world's resources and create 25 percent of the world's air pollution, we bear a greater responsibility for taking the international lead in addressing these problems.

Choice Three says we must fall into step with Nature – that we can no longer reroute rivers to farm deserts, completely eliminate the summer with air conditioners, or drive bigger and bigger cars and vans. The average American uses more energy than three Japanese – or an entire village of 422 Ethiopians – according to United Nations statistics. We make up less than 5 percent of the world's population, yet we consume nearly 30 percent of the global resources available each year. Directly or indirectly, every American consumes his or her weight in natural resources every day, or 23 times more than the world average. Over one lifetime, the average American produces 52 tons of garbage and 412 tons of carbon dioxide.

Not only do these statistics suggest that consumption and emission levels should go down, they also suggest that these levels will go down, because the Earth cannot sustain them indefinitely, says Donella Meadows, a professor of environmental studies at Dartmouth College. The stark choice, she says, is whether we reduce them deliberately or wait until they fall on their own with the collapse of ecological and social systems.

## We're Changing the Climate

The insurance industry, which takes a strictly dollars-and-cents approach to this or any issue, is sponsoring extensive research about global warming and is scaling back coverage in vulnerable areas like Florida. By 2010, according to Travelers Insurance Corp., global warming could extend the hurricane season by 20 days and increase storm-related losses by 30 percent. "The insurance business is first in line to be affected by climate change," Franklin Nutter, president of the Reinsurance Association of America, testified in a 1994 congressional hearing. "It could bankrupt the industry."

> The average American uses more energy than three Japanese — or an entire village of 422 Ethiopians — according to United Nations statistics.

## What Can Be Done?

### Supporters of Choice Three generally favor the following measures:

■ Due to the environmental threats facing us, we must give environmental protection the highest priority in public policy and funding.

■ Government must make it a national priority to wean the nation from air-polluting fossil fuels, replacing them with natural gas and solar power. To reduce the production and use of environmentally unsafe products, we must increase taxes on such things as coal, oil, gasoline, pesticides, and toxic waste.

■ To fall into step with Nature, Americans must accept changes in their lifestyle that reduce the life-threatening strain we put on the environment. Among other things, we need to drive less, join car pools, and use fans instead of air conditioners.

■ Government must strengthen auto emissions standards and increase subsidies for public transportation. The U.S. must live up to its promise, made in a 1992 United Nations agreement, to freeze carbon dioxide emissions at their 1990 levels by 2000.

■ Government should develop conservation plans for ecosystems in every region. We must protect species and habitats that are already threatened, and prevent damage to others.

■ Environmental regulations must increasingly focus on preventing pollution problems from getting started rather than on managing them after they develop.

■ As both the world's political and pollution leader, the U.S. should take the lead in solving international problems such as global warming, acid rain, and the loss of stratospheric ozone.

Global warming, once just a theme in science fiction, still seemed far-fetched to many people until October 1995, when the UN published a landmark report by its Intergovernmental Panel on Climate Change, an international brain trust of 2,500 climate experts. The report seemed to end the debate about whether consumption and pollution levels can change the climate, stating unequivocally: "A pattern of climatic response to human activities is identifiable in the climatological record."

Global temperatures have increased by 1 degree Fahrenheit in the last century and, accelerated by rising concentrations of air pollution, temperatures could increase by 2 to 6 degrees by the year 2100, the panel said. A 2-degree increase would play considerable havoc with the climate, and a 6-degree increase would

## A Glimpse of Global Warming?
## Recent weather-related disasters

| Disaster | Location | Date | Number of deaths | Estimated damages (billions of dollars) |
|---|---|---|---|---|
| Windstorm Daria | Europe | Jan. 1990 | n/a | $4.6 |
| Windstorm Vivian | Europe | Feb. 1990 | n/a | $3.2 |
| Unnamed cyclone | Bangladesh | May 1991 | 140,000 | $3.0 |
| Flood | China | Summer 1991 | 3,074 | $15.0 |
| Typhoon Mireille | Japan | Sept. 1991 | 62 | $6.0 |
| Hurricane Andrew | North America | Aug. 1992 | 74 | $30.0 |
| Cyclone Iniki | North America | Aug. 1992 | 4 | $3.0 |
| Winter storm | North America | March 1993 | 246 | $5.0 |
| Mississippi floods | North America | July/Aug. 1993 | 41 | $12.0 |
| Winter damage | North America | Jan. 1994 | 170 | $4.0 |
| Spring floods | China | Spring 1994 | 1,846 | $7.8 |
| Flood | Italy | Nov. 1994 | 64 | $9.3 |
| Winter floods | Northern Europe | Jan./Feb. 1995 | 28 | $3.5 |

Source: Gerhard A. Berz, Munich Reinsurance Company, Munich, Germany

## Diminishing Virgin Forests

Colored areas represent locations of the ancient forests in the contiguous 48 states

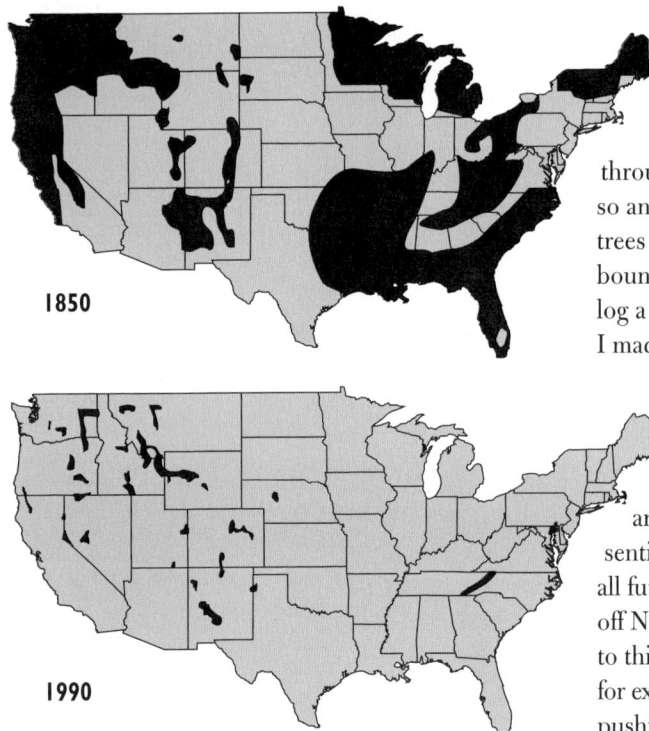

1850

1990

Source: Adapted from Seth Zuckerman, *Saving Our Ancient Forests* (Los Angeles: Living Planet Press, 1991)

reshape the planet, with new wind and rain patterns, rising seas, lengthening droughts, and more violent floods and hurricanes, the panel said. In the U.S., global warming would regularly bring killer storms and floods, submerge coastal areas, dry out forests, cause the evaporation of drinking water, exacerbate air pollution, and cause droughts in the South and Midwest.

The longer we wait to respond, the higher the likely costs and risks of global warming, the UN panel said. As first steps, the scientists recommended planting forests, making buildings and cars much more energy-efficient, expanding public transportation, and requiring all new factories and utilities to use natural gas or solar energy instead of coal or oil. Choice Three supporters call for the nation to make this environmental transformation a national priority, putting it on the fastest possible track. An economic dividend of this approach is that it would position the U.S. as the world's leading exporter of environmentally safe technologies.

### Saving Nature

Brock Evans, vice president of the National Audubon Society, tells how a family walk in an ancient forest in Washington changed his life.

"We stepped out of the car that bright Sunday morning and immediately into a hushed cathedral of a forest, row upon row of giant, massed trunks six to eight feet thick, several hundred feet high. We walked through this magnificence for a hundred yards or so and I noticed a yellow sign on one of the big trees and went over to look. It said, 'clear-cut boundary – U.S. Forest Service.' Who would ever log a place like this? My eyes filled with tears, and I made a vow to myself that I would give the rest of my life, whatever it took, to try to put an end to the destruction of something so magnificent as our Northwest forest."

Ninety-five percent of the Northwest's ancient forest has now vanished, he says, representing an incalculable loss to all Americans and all future generations. Not only is it immoral to kill off Nature, it's not good for our health, according to this view. As loggers harvested the Douglas fir, for example, they discarded scraggly yew trees, pushing the species toward extinction before scientists discovered that yew bark provides a chemical substance called Taxol, one of the best treatments for breast and ovarian cancers. "The fact is that, in the end, the Endangered Species Act is really about people," Evans says. Half of our medicines and nearly all of our antibiotics are derived from wild organisms, most of them glamourless microbes and species like toads, fireflies, and the Madagascar periwinkle – a plant that helps children survive leukemia.

The plight of individual species, however, is itself dwarfed by the plight of entire ecosystems, according to a 1995 federal study by the National Biological Service. In this first-ever review of the entire American landscape, scientists reported that natural habitats on at least half the nation's land have deteriorated to the point of endangerment. "The time is ripe for a concerted effort to identify and protect ecosystems across the United States," the scientists concluded. Supporters of Choice Three agree.

## The River Runs Dry

The environment is dying of thirst, according to this view. Farmers, industries, and consumers use and waste so much water that little remains to sustain waterways and aquatic species. The mighty Colorado, the most important river in the Southwest, runs dry miles before its ancient bed reaches the sea at the Gulf of California. Controlled by 10 dams, including the Hoover, it irrigates 2 million acres of farmland, fills swimming pools as far away as Hollywood, and powers the neon strip in Las Vegas as well as homes in seven states. Compacts among the various jurisdictions that divvy up the Colorado leave no flow to sustain the river itself, endangering scores of species and even a tribe of Mexican Indians who have made their living on the river for 2,000 years. Known as the Cucapa, or "the people of the river," in some seasons they no longer have a river, never mind fish, and only about 40 families remain. "Barring a miracle, you're seeing the last of them," Anita Alvarez de Williams, an anthropologist, told *National Geographic*.

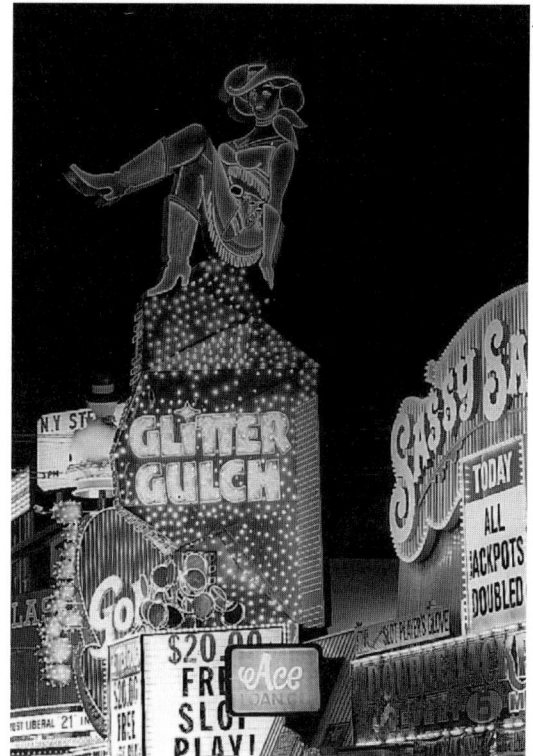

A symbol of the abuse of nature, the Colorado River runs dry miles before it reaches the sea. Among other things, the river's hydroelectric plants fuel Las Vegas' neon strip.

Demand for water exceeds the nation's supply and threatens countless aquatic ecosystems. In this view, becoming better environmental stewards means consuming less and giving more back to the environment – for our own good.

## Medicinal Plants: Cures that Nature provides

Medicines derived from plants or synthesized medicines based on plants

| Medicinal use | Medicine | Plant |
| --- | --- | --- |
| Cancer, especially breast and ovarian cancers | Taxol | Pacific yew tree |
| Cancer, especially Hodgkins disease and leukemia | Vincristine and vinblastine | Rosy periwinkle |
| Heart disease | Digitalis | Foxglove |
| Hypertension | Reserpine | Snakeroot |
| Analgesic and cough suppressant | Codeine | Opium poppy |
| Analgesic | Morphine | Opium poppy |
| Analgesic | Aspirin | White willow |
| Oral contraception | Diosgenins | Wild yam |
| Surgical anesthetic | Tubocurarine | Curare vine |

Sources: Michael Balick et al,. *Medicinal Resources of the Tropical Forest* (New York: Columbia University Press, 1996); Patricia Brynes, "Wild Medicine," *Wilderness* (Fall 1995); Steven Foster and James Duke, *A Field Guide to Medicinal Plants* (Boston: Houghton Mifflin, 1990); Cathy Sears, "Jungle Potions," *American Health* (October 1992).

## In Support

✓ Saving the planet and protecting our health must take precedence over all other public problems. Nature has its limits, both in its ability to absorb pollution and to regenerate. We must act aggressively to deal with existing problems and prevent worse problems from occurring later on.

✓ Globally, species are being killed off at the rate of 100 a day, by one estimate. This represents an incalculable loss of biologic diversity, which threatens the health of the planet and everyone on it.

✓ It is also our moral obligation to protect endangered species. "The Endangered Species Act is the Noah's Ark of our day," says Dr. Calvin B. Dewitt, a founder of the Evangelical Environmental Network.

✓ The bottom line for the green approach to the environment is black. For example, a study by four environmental groups in 1992 concluded that aggressive efforts to reduce carbon dioxide emissions by 70 percent over 40 years would cost about $2.7 trillion, but would yield $5 trillion in savings to consumers and industry, producing a net gain of $2.3 trillion. Also, dealing with our own problems will put the U.S. in a position to become the leading exporter of environmentally safe technology.

✓ The U.S. has both a responsibility and a selfish interest in taking the lead in protecting the global environment. For one thing, we produce 25 percent of the world's air pollution. For another, we'll be breathing more pollution from developing nations if we don't help solve this global problem.

## In Opposition

✓ This approach overestimates environmental dangers and overreacts with a plan that elevates environmental concerns above all others. Supporters of this alarmist approach have previously predicted disasters that did not occur.

✓ Meteorologists have trouble making accurate five-day forecasts, never mind predicting climate changes in 50 or 100 years. Scientists disagree about what may be causing global warming, what we can do to stop it, or even what effect it will have. Developing strategies now would be wasteful.

✓ The dramatic shifts in taxes, consumption, manufacturing, and employment that this approach calls for would needlessly disrupt the nation and cause enormous hardship for many Americans.

✓ This kind of approach attempts the impossible: it tries to halt evolution by preserving ecosystems at a certain time, according to 46 prominent American scientists, including 27 Nobel Prize winners. In a 1992 letter to the United Nations, they wrote that Nature is dynamic, random, and evolutionary: "We contend that a Natural State, sometimes idealized by movements with a tendency to look toward the past, does not exist and has probably never existed."

✓ Even if we could do it, we could not afford to protect every living thing that swims, crawls, or photosynthesizes. So far, costly government efforts to protect endangered species and habitats have yielded poor results: since 1973, seven listed species became extinct and seven others were removed, most because additional populations were discovered.

Niculae Asciu

### For Further Reading /
Working Toward a Sustainable Environment

■ Paul and Anne Ehrlich, *Healing the Planet: Strategies for Resolving the Environmental Crisis* (Reading, Mass.: Addison-Wesley Publishing Company, 1991).

■ Al Gore, *Earth in the Balance: Ecology and the Human Spirit* (Boston: Houghton Mifflin Company, 1992).

■ C. Silver and R. Defries, eds., *One Earth, One Future: Our Changing Global Environment* (Washington, D.C.: National Academy Press, 1990).

# One Step Forward, Two Steps Back?

It's hard to tell whether we're making much environmental progress. One step forward: American Express reduced its electric bills by installing an energy-efficient lighting system in its 51-story headquarters in New York. Area residents also benefited by not having to breathe 3,300 tons of air pollution annually, which utilities would otherwise have generated to power a conventional lighting system in the AmEx tower.

Two steps back: the 1,400 sports utility vehicles that roll off one manufacturer's assembly line every day will release more than 6,600 tons of pollutants a year into the air. Americans are driving bigger vehicles longer distances at higher speeds, and they're fueling cars and trucks with gasoline that costs less than many brands of bottled water.

Is this a problem? If so, what's the solution? Consider three approaches to this situation:

Choice One says cleaning up the environment requires stricter standards for fuel efficiency and pollution control, and better enforcement of those standards. Choice Two says it is impractical to raise fuel-efficiency standards, because it would be exorbitantly expensive and the reduction in pollution would be marginal. Choice Three argues for taking a giant step beyond Choice One, calling on government to increase subsidies for public transportation and taxes on gasoline and gas-guzzlers, and calling on the American public to make major lifestyle changes such as leaving cars at home and using mass transit instead.

This issue book presents three major approaches to environmental protection, but leaves the reader with the tough job of making a choice and accepting tradeoffs. Not all the choices are mutually exclusive, but each approaches the problem and solution in a fundamentally different way. Some questions to focus discussion:

■ **What do you value most?** Choice One calls for strengthening laws and enforcement to speed environmental progress. Choice Two says regulations have already gone too far, and instead calls for incentives that encourage people to protect the environment. Choice Three calls for government to act aggressively to prevent pollution and reduce consumption of environmentally unsafe products.

■ **How much are you concerned about environmental problems?** Choice One says they are serious, but manageable. Choice Two says many environmental concerns are exaggerated; we have made considerable headway, and will make more progress as people are given more responsibility. Choice Three says environmental threats dwarf other concerns now facing the nation and must take precedence.

■ **What role should government play?** Choice One says government plays an essential role in setting and enforcing environmental standards. Choice Two says that the role of government should be greatly reduced, and the role of citizens and property owners increased. Choice Three says government must aggressively wean industries and consumers away from environmentally unsafe practices, products, and lifestyles.

■ **Can you accept the tradeoffs?** Choice One, in advocating flexible regulations to save money, would allow regional differences in the way industries meet national pollution goals; consequently, some areas of the nation would be more polluted than others. Choice Two, in relying on ordinary citizens to stop polluters with lawsuits, would shift many enforcement responsibilities and costs to individuals. Choice Three, in calling for Americans to consume less and waste less, would require major lifestyle adjustments, including changes in transportation, employment, and family budgets.

# Comparing the Choices

The vast majority of Americans consider themselves environmentalists, sharing common values as well as many concerns about wildlife, water, air, and land. But there are fundamental differences in how we propose to address environmental challenges. As state and federal officials consider legislation governing the environment, citizens can help shape the public debate by considering three major approaches to environmental protection.

Niculae Asciu

## Choice 1

### Strengthening Laws and Enforcement

We've made a lot of progress in protecting the environment, but now we need stronger laws and better enforcement to continue the job.

### What Can Be Done?
- Increase funding for the U.S. Environmental Protection Agency.
- Increase enforcement of regulations, especially those dealing with high risks.
- Make regulations strict but flexible, to get the most protection for the money.

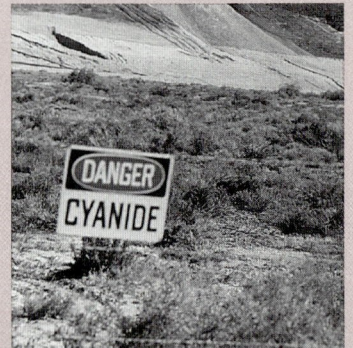

### In Support
- We've made much progress in 25 years, but much more needs to be done.
- Enforcement of many environmental regulations is feeble, and should be strengthened.
- Government is best at setting environmental standards; business is best at developing the least costly way to comply.

### In Opposition
- This approach calls for more regulations, which, in one view, is exactly the reverse of what is needed: deregulation.
- Most of the nation's environmental problems have already been solved or are being solved.
- In another view, this approach falls short because it fails to address global environmental threats meaningfully.

### A Likely Tradeoff
- In calling for stricter regulations, this approach would increase costs for businesses and consumers.

## Choice 2

### Using Incentives, Not Regulations

We must eliminate costly regulations that abuse property rights yet produce poor environmental results.

### What Can Be Done?

- Reduce, to the minimum, government's role in regulating the environment.
- Provide incentives, not penalties, to protect the environment.
- Compensate property owners when it's necessary to take their property for public uses.

### In Support

- Excessive regulation is hurting the economy and producing few environmental benefits.
- What works best in America is the market-place; let it protect the environment.
- There is no better environmental steward than the property owner, who has a keen self-interest in protecting its value.

### In Opposition

- Government must protect the environment precisely because it was deteriorating without regulations.
- This approach wrongly suggests that citizens can take the place of regulatory agencies in stopping polluters.
- Studies show that environmental rules have a small, but positive, effect on employment.

### A Likely Tradeoff

- In relying on private lawsuits to stop polluters, this approach would shift enforcement costs and responsibilities to citizens.

## Choice 3

### Working Toward a Sustainable Environment

To protect our lives and our planet, we must eliminate environmentally unsafe practices, products, and lifestyles.

### What Can Be Done?

- Reduce pollution and consumption to levels that can be sustained indefinitely.
- Prevent pollution rather than simply trying to clean it up after it occurs.
- Raise taxes on such things as coal, oil, gasoline, pesticides, and toxic waste.

### In Support

- We only have one planet, with a limited supply of natural resources and a limited ability to absorb pollution.
- It's our moral obligation to use natural resources in a way that can be sustained, generation after generation.
- Preventive measures are more effective and less costly in the long run than responding to each environmental crisis as it emerges.

### In Opposition

- This approach overestimates environmental dangers and overreacts.
- This choice ignores Nature's dynamic, random, and evolutionary properties.
- This approach calls for unnecessary changes in industry, employment, and lifestyles – all of which would create hardship for most Americans.

### A Likely Tradeoff

- In calling for society to switch to environmentally safe products and behaviors, this approach would radically change American lifestyles.

# What Are the National Issues Forums?

National Issues Forums provide opportunities for citizens around the nation to gather and discuss the most challenging social issues of the day. Forums have focused on such issues as the economy, education, healthcare, and crime. The forums are organized by thousands of civic, service, and religious organizations as well as by libraries, high schools, and colleges.

Having together helped select discussion topics from among the year's most pressing public concerns, these sponsoring organizations design and coordinate their own forum programs each fall and winter. No two forums are alike. They vary in size from small study circles to large forums modeled after traditional town meetings, but they are all different from both everyday conversations and adversarial debates. Forums present each issue in a neutral, nonpartisan way that encourages people to take a fresh look at the topic and at their own convictions. Here are some answers to frequently asked questions:

**Can I participate if I haven't followed the topic closely?** Absolutely. The forums are intended to increase public understanding of complicated topics. Forum conveners distribute issue books, which provide a nonpartisan overview of each topic and several alternative choices or courses of action that address the issue.

**What happens in forums?** In the forums, participants share their opinions, their concerns, and their knowledge. With the help of moderators and the framework for discussion contained in the issue books, participants weigh several possible ways for our society to address a given problem. Participants analyze each of their choices, the arguments for and against them, and discuss the tradeoffs and other implications. Forum moderators encourage participants to examine their values as individuals and as community members.

**Isn't one person's opinion as good as another's?** Moderators encourage participants to discuss their attitudes, concerns, and convictions about each issue and, as a group, to sort out their conflicting priorities. In this way, participants move from making individual choices to making choices as a group.

Forums enrich participants' thinking about public issues. Participants confront the issue head-on, make an informed decision about how to address it, and come to terms with the likely consequences of their choices. In this deliberative process, participants often accept choices that are not entirely consistent with what they want, and impose costs and consequences that they had not initially considered. This happens because forums help people see issues from different points of view: forum participants use the discussion process to discover, rather than to persuade or advocate. Deliberative forums, at their best, can help participants move toward shared, stable, well-informed public judgments about important public issues.

**Are participants expected to agree on a course of action?** Forums provide a framework for people to find the areas where their interests and goals overlap. In a democracy, citizens must come together and find answers they can all live with – while acknowledging that individuals have differing opinions. Forums enable this to happen and allow a public voice to emerge that can give direction to public policy.

It is important to remember that this direction is devised by the public – the forum participants. National Issues Forums are nonpartisan and do not advocate a particular solution to any public issue.

National Issues Forums are not to be confused with referenda or public opinion polls. Rather, they enable diverse groups of citizens to determine together what direction they want policy to take, what kinds of action and legislation they favor, and what, for their common good, they resist.

**Do forums lead to political action?** Forums can lead to several kinds of political action. Each year, results of the forums are shared with people in public office, and in this way, forum participants help set the government's compass. Sometimes, too, individuals, as a result of attending forums, decide what they can do personally. Forums may also lead to complementary actions, as individuals and groups decide which portions of a public problem they can remedy.

---

**Want to start a forum?**

Forums are initiated at the local level by civic and educational organizations. For information about starting a forum and using our materials, write the NIF Institute, P.O. Box 75306, Washington, D.C. 20013-5306, or phone 800-433-7834.

**NATIONAL ISSUES FORUMS**

# Environmental Protection
## A Challenge Bigger Than All Outdoors

One of the reasons people participate in the National Issues Forums is that they want leaders to know how they feel about the issues. So that we can present your thoughts and feelings about this issue, we'd like you to fill out this ballot before you attend forum meetings (or before you read this book, if you buy it elsewhere), and to fill out a second ballot after the forum (or after you've read the material). Before answering these questions, make up a three-digit number and enter it in the box below.

    The moderator of your local forum will ask you to hand in this ballot at the end of the session. If you cannot attend the meeting, send the completed ballot to: The National Issues Forums Research, 100 Commons Road, Dayton, Ohio 45459-2777.

**Fill in your three-digit number here.**

**1.** Here is a list on which proposals to protect the environment might be based. How important do you think each one should be in making policy about the environment?

| | Very important | Somewhat important | Not at all important | Not sure |
|---|---|---|---|---|
| **a.** Government must take the lead in making and enforcing laws to protect the environment. | ☐ | ☐ | ☐ | ☐ |
| **b.** We should set strict standards, but let businesses decide how to meet them. | ☐ | ☐ | ☐ | ☐ |
| **c.** Responsibility for clean air and water should be in the hands of private businesses and landowners. | ☐ | ☐ | ☐ | ☐ |
| **d.** Programs to protect the environment should address worldwide concerns such as global warming. | ☐ | ☐ | ☐ | ☐ |
| **e.** Government should pay property owners when it restricts the use of their land. | ☐ | ☐ | ☐ | ☐ |
| **f.** We should encourage the use of fuels that do not pollute the environment. | ☐ | ☐ | ☐ | ☐ |

**2.** Look at Question #1 again. How strongly is each principle reflected in our current efforts to protect the environment?

| | Strongly | Somewhat strongly | Not at all | Not sure |
|---|---|---|---|---|
| **a.** Government must take the lead in making and enforcing laws to protect the environment. | ☐ | ☐ | ☐ | ☐ |
| **b.** We should set strict standards, but let businesses decide how to meet them. | ☐ | ☐ | ☐ | ☐ |
| **c.** Responsibility for clean air and water should be in the hands of private businesses and landowners. | ☐ | ☐ | ☐ | ☐ |
| **d.** Programs to protect the environment should address worldwide concerns such as global warming. | ☐ | ☐ | ☐ | ☐ |
| **e.** Government should pay property owners when it restricts the use of their land. | ☐ | ☐ | ☐ | ☐ |
| **f.** We should encourage the use of fuels that do not pollute the environment. | ☐ | ☐ | ☐ | ☐ |

**3.** Are there any other principles that you think should guide our policy on the environment? Please explain.

_____

_____

_____

**4.** How concerned are you about the following?

| | Very concerned | Somewhat concerned | Not at all concerned | Not sure |
|---|---|---|---|---|
| **a.** Giving away public lands to loggers, miners, and other private interests. | ☐ | ☐ | ☐ | ☐ |
| **b.** The dangers of global warming. | ☐ | ☐ | ☐ | ☐ |
| **c.** Too much environmental regulation is smothering economic growth. | ☐ | ☐ | ☐ | ☐ |
| **d.** Not getting our money's worth from costly environmental programs. | ☐ | ☐ | ☐ | ☐ |
| **e.** Wasting energy resources that cannot be replaced. | ☐ | ☐ | ☐ | ☐ |
| **f.** Environmental programs that are more concerned with animals and plants than with people. | ☐ | ☐ | ☐ | ☐ |

*Continued on next page*

**5.** Do you have any other concerns about programs to protect the environment? Please explain.

_____

_____

_____

_____

| 6. How do you feel about these approaches to protecting the environment? | Favor | Oppose | Not sure |
|---|---|---|---|
| **a.** We must enact tougher laws to protect the environment EVEN IF this may be hard on many businesses. | ☐ | ☐ | ☐ |
| **b.** We must reduce the government's role in protecting the environment EVEN IF that means depending on property owners to do the job. | ☐ | ☐ | ☐ |
| **c.** We must take steps to control global warming EVEN IF Americans will have to pay more for, and use less of, some products. | ☐ | ☐ | ☐ |

**7.** Which statement best describes how you feel? (Please mark only one.)

**a.** I am not sure what should be done to change environmental protection laws. ☐

**b.** I have a general idea of what changes should be made. ☐

**c.** I have a clear, definite idea of what changes should be made. ☐

# Environmental Protection
## A Challenge Bigger Than All Outdoors

Now that you've had a chance to read the book or attend a forum discussion, we'd like to know what you think about this issue. Your opinions, along with those of thousands of others who participated in this year's forums, will be reflected in a summary report prepared for participants as well as elected officials and policymakers working on this problem. Since we're interested in whether you have changed your mind about certain aspects of this issue, the questions are the same as those you answered earlier. Before answering the questions, please write in the box below the same three-digit number you used for the Pre-Forum Ballot.

Please hand this ballot to the forum leader at the end of the session, or mail it to: The National Issues Forums Research, 100 Commons Road, Dayton, Ohio 45459-2777.

**Fill in your three-digit number here.**

1. Here is a list on which proposals to protect the environment might be based. How important do you think each one should be in making policy about the environment?

| | Very important | Somewhat important | Not at all important | Not sure |
|---|---|---|---|---|
| a. Government must take the lead in making and enforcing laws to protect the environment. | ☐ | ☐ | ☐ | ☐ |
| b. We should set strict standards, but let businesses decide how to meet them. | ☐ | ☐ | ☐ | ☐ |
| c. Responsibility for clean air and water should be in the hands of private businesses and landowners. | ☐ | ☐ | ☐ | ☐ |
| d. Programs to protect the environment should address worldwide concerns such as global warming. | ☐ | ☐ | ☐ | ☐ |
| e. Government should pay property owners when it restricts the use of their land. | ☐ | ☐ | ☐ | ☐ |
| f. We should encourage the use of fuels that do not pollute the environment. | ☐ | ☐ | ☐ | ☐ |

2. Look at Question #1 again. How strongly is each principle reflected in our current efforts to protect the environment?

| | Strongly | Somewhat strongly | Not at all | Not sure |
|---|---|---|---|---|
| a. Government must take the lead in making and enforcing laws to protect the environment. | ☐ | ☐ | ☐ | ☐ |
| b. We should set strict standards, but let businesses decide how to meet them. | ☐ | ☐ | ☐ | ☐ |
| c. Responsibility for clean air and water should be in the hands of private businesses and landowners. | ☐ | ☐ | ☐ | ☐ |
| d. Programs to protect the environment should address worldwide concerns such as global warming. | ☐ | ☐ | ☐ | ☐ |
| e. Government should pay property owners when it restricts the use of their land. | ☐ | ☐ | ☐ | ☐ |
| f. We should encourage the use of fuels that do not pollute the environment. | ☐ | ☐ | ☐ | ☐ |

3. Are there any other principles that you think should guide our policy on the environment? Please explain.

_____

_____

_____

4. How concerned are you about the following?

| | Very concerned | Somewhat concerned | Not at all concerned | Not sure |
|---|---|---|---|---|
| a. Giving away public lands to loggers, miners, and other private interests. | ☐ | ☐ | ☐ | ☐ |
| b. The dangers of global warming. | ☐ | ☐ | ☐ | ☐ |
| c. Too much environmental regulation is smothering economic growth. | ☐ | ☐ | ☐ | ☐ |
| d. Not getting our money's worth from costly environmental programs. | ☐ | ☐ | ☐ | ☐ |
| e. Wasting energy resources that cannot be replaced. | ☐ | ☐ | ☐ | ☐ |
| f. Environmental programs that are more concerned with animals and plants than with people. | ☐ | ☐ | ☐ | ☐ |

*Continued on next page*

**5.** Do you have any other concerns about programs to protect the environment? Please explain.

_____

_____

_____

_____

**6.** How do you feel about these approaches to protecting the environment?

| | Favor | Oppose | Not sure |
|---|---|---|---|
| **a.** We must enact tougher laws to protect the environment EVEN IF this may be hard on many businesses. | ☐ | ☐ | ☐ |
| **b.** We must reduce the government's role in protecting the environment EVEN IF that means depending on property owners to do the job. | ☐ | ☐ | ☐ |
| **c.** We must take steps to control global warming EVEN IF Americans will have to pay more for, and use less of, some products. | ☐ | ☐ | ☐ |

**7.** Which statement best describes how you feel? (Please mark only one.)

**a.** I am not sure what should be done to change environmental protection laws. ☐

**b.** I have a general idea of what changes should be made. ☐

**c.** I have a clear, definite idea of what changes should be made. ☐